50 Greek Kitchen: A Taste of the Mediterranean Recipes

By: Kelly Johnson

Table of Contents

- Moussaka (Layered Eggplant and Meat Casserole)
- Pastitsio (Greek Baked Pasta with Meat and Béchamel)
- Spanakopita (Spinach and Feta Pie)
- Tiropita (Cheese Pie)
- Horiatiki (Greek Village Salad)
- Tzatziki (Yogurt and Cucumber Dip)
- Skordalia (Garlic Potato Dip)
- Melitzanosalata (Eggplant Dip)
- Taramosalata (Fish Roe Spread)
- Dolmades (Stuffed Grape Leaves)
- Gigantes Plaki (Baked Giant Beans)
- Fasolada (Greek White Bean Soup)
- Avgolemono Soup (Lemon and Egg Chicken Soup)
- Psarosoupa (Greek Fish Soup)
- Youvetsi (Beef or Lamb with Orzo)
- Stifado (Greek Beef Stew with Onions)
- Soutzoukakia (Greek Meatballs in Tomato Sauce)
- Keftedes (Greek Meatballs)
- Souvlaki (Grilled Meat Skewers)
- Gyros (Pita-Wrapped Meat with Tzatziki)
- Kokkinisto (Greek Braised Meat in Tomato Sauce)
- Kleftiko (Slow-Cooked Lamb)
- Arni me Patates (Roast Lamb with Potatoes)
- Psito Kotopoulo (Greek Roast Chicken)
- Bakaliaros Skordalia (Fried Cod with Garlic Sauce)
- Xtapodi Stifado (Octopus Stew)
- Garides Saganaki (Shrimp in Tomato and Feta Sauce)
- Midia Saganaki (Mussels in Tomato and Feta Sauce)
- Briam (Greek Ratatouille)
- Imam Bayildi (Stuffed Eggplant)
- Gemista (Stuffed Tomatoes and Peppers)
- Fasolia Yiahni (Braised Green Beans in Tomato Sauce)
- Horta Vrasta (Boiled Wild Greens with Olive Oil and Lemon)
- Revithia Sto Fourno (Baked Chickpeas)
- Melomakarona (Honey-Dipped Spiced Cookies)

- Kourabiedes (Greek Butter Cookies with Powdered Sugar)
- Loukoumades (Greek Honey Puffs)
- Baklava (Layered Phyllo Pastry with Nuts and Honey)
- Galaktoboureko (Custard Phyllo Pie)
- Bougatsa (Greek Custard or Cheese Pastry)
- Kataifi (Shredded Phyllo Dessert with Nuts and Syrup)
- Rizogalo (Greek Rice Pudding)
- Halva (Semolina or Tahini-Based Dessert)
- Portokalopita (Orange Phyllo Cake)
- Tsoureki (Greek Sweet Bread)
- Diples (Fried Pastry with Honey and Nuts)
- Karydopita (Greek Walnut Cake with Syrup)
- Avgofetes (Greek-Style French Toast)
- Ouzo Spritz (Greek Aperitif Cocktail)
- Ellinikos Kafes (Traditional Greek Coffee)

Moussaka (Layered Eggplant and Meat Casserole)

A rich and comforting Greek casserole with eggplant, ground meat, and béchamel sauce.

Ingredients:

- 2 eggplants, sliced
- 1 lb ground beef or lamb
- 1 onion, chopped
- 2 cloves garlic, minced
- 1 can (14 oz) crushed tomatoes
- 1 tsp cinnamon
- Salt and pepper
- ½ cup red wine
- 2 tbsp olive oil

Béchamel Sauce:

- 2 tbsp butter
- 2 tbsp flour
- 2 cups milk
- 1 egg yolk
- ½ cup grated Parmesan

Instructions:

1. Salt eggplant slices and let sit for 30 minutes. Rinse and pat dry.
2. Fry eggplant slices in olive oil until golden.
3. Sauté onion and garlic, then add ground meat. Cook until browned.
4. Add tomatoes, wine, cinnamon, salt, and pepper. Simmer for 20 minutes.
5. For béchamel, melt butter, whisk in flour, then slowly add milk. Cook until thickened, then whisk in egg yolk and Parmesan.
6. In a baking dish, layer eggplant and meat sauce, then top with béchamel.
7. Bake at 375°F (190°C) for 40 minutes until golden.

Pastitsio (Greek Baked Pasta with Meat and Béchamel)

A hearty layered Greek pasta dish similar to lasagna but with a creamy béchamel topping.

Ingredients:

- 12 oz penne or bucatini pasta
- 1 lb ground beef or lamb
- 1 onion, chopped
- 1 clove garlic, minced
- 1 can (14 oz) crushed tomatoes
- 1 tsp cinnamon
- ½ cup red wine
- ½ cup grated Kefalotyri or Parmesan cheese

Béchamel Sauce:

- 2 tbsp butter
- 2 tbsp flour
- 2 cups milk
- 1 egg yolk
- ½ cup grated cheese

Instructions:

1. Cook pasta, drain, and toss with a little butter.
2. Sauté onion and garlic, then add meat and brown. Add tomatoes, wine, cinnamon, salt, and pepper. Simmer for 20 minutes.
3. Prepare béchamel as in the Moussaka recipe.
4. In a baking dish, layer half the pasta, meat sauce, remaining pasta, then top with béchamel and cheese.
5. Bake at 375°F (190°C) for 40 minutes until golden.

Spanakopita (Spinach and Feta Pie)

A crispy and flaky pastry filled with spinach and feta cheese.

Ingredients:

- 1 lb spinach, chopped
- 1 onion, chopped
- 2 cloves garlic, minced
- ½ cup feta cheese, crumbled
- 2 eggs, beaten
- 1 tsp dill
- 8 sheets phyllo dough
- ½ cup butter or olive oil

Instructions:

1. Sauté onion and garlic in olive oil. Add spinach and cook until wilted.
2. Remove from heat and mix in feta, eggs, and dill.
3. Brush a baking dish with butter and layer 4 sheets of phyllo, brushing each with butter.
4. Spread filling, then cover with 4 more buttered phyllo sheets.
5. Bake at 375°F (190°C) for 30 minutes until golden.

Tiropita (Cheese Pie)

A deliciously cheesy Greek pastry wrapped in flaky phyllo dough.

Ingredients:

- 1 cup feta cheese, crumbled
- ½ cup ricotta cheese
- 1 egg, beaten
- 8 sheets phyllo dough
- ½ cup melted butter

Instructions:

1. Mix cheeses and egg.
2. Cut phyllo sheets into strips, brush with butter, and place a spoonful of filling on one end.
3. Fold into triangles and place on a baking sheet.
4. Bake at 375°F (190°C) for 20 minutes until golden.

Horiatiki (Greek Village Salad)

A fresh and simple Greek salad with tomatoes, cucumbers, and feta.

Ingredients:

- 2 tomatoes, chopped
- 1 cucumber, sliced
- ½ red onion, thinly sliced
- ½ cup Kalamata olives
- 4 oz feta cheese
- 2 tbsp olive oil
- 1 tbsp red wine vinegar
- 1 tsp oregano
- Salt and pepper

Instructions:

1. Combine vegetables and olives in a bowl.
2. Drizzle with olive oil and vinegar, then season with oregano, salt, and pepper.
3. Top with feta and serve.

Tzatziki (Yogurt and Cucumber Dip)

A cool and creamy dip perfect for grilled meats or pita bread.

Ingredients:

- 1 cup Greek yogurt
- ½ cucumber, grated and drained
- 1 clove garlic, minced
- 1 tbsp olive oil
- 1 tsp lemon juice
- 1 tsp dill
- Salt

Instructions:

1. Mix all ingredients in a bowl.
2. Chill before serving.

Skordalia (Garlic Potato Dip)

A thick and garlicky Greek dip often served with bread or fried fish.

Ingredients:

- 2 potatoes, boiled and mashed
- 4 cloves garlic, minced
- ¼ cup olive oil
- 2 tbsp lemon juice
- Salt

Instructions:

1. Blend all ingredients until smooth.
2. Serve at room temperature.

Melitzanosalata (Eggplant Dip)

A smoky and creamy roasted eggplant dip.

Ingredients:

- 1 large eggplant
- 1 clove garlic, minced
- 2 tbsp olive oil
- 1 tbsp lemon juice
- ½ tsp salt

Instructions:

1. Roast eggplant until soft. Scoop out flesh and mash.
2. Mix with garlic, olive oil, lemon juice, and salt.

Taramosalata (Fish Roe Spread)

A creamy and tangy Greek dip made with fish roe and bread.

Ingredients:

- ¼ cup tarama (fish roe)
- 2 slices bread, soaked in water and squeezed dry
- ½ cup olive oil
- 1 tbsp lemon juice

Instructions:

1. Blend all ingredients until smooth.
2. Chill before serving.

Dolmades (Stuffed Grape Leaves)

Grape leaves filled with a savory rice mixture, often served with lemon sauce.

Ingredients:

- 1 jar grape leaves, rinsed
- 1 cup rice
- 1 onion, finely chopped
- 2 tbsp olive oil
- ½ cup fresh herbs (dill, mint, parsley), chopped
- 1 lemon, juiced
- Salt and pepper

Instructions:

1. Sauté onion in olive oil, then mix with rice, herbs, salt, and pepper.
2. Place a spoonful of filling on each grape leaf, roll tightly.
3. Arrange in a pot, cover with water and lemon juice, and simmer for 45 minutes.

Gigantes Plaki (Baked Giant Beans)

Large white beans baked in a rich tomato sauce.

Ingredients:

- 2 cups giant beans (soaked overnight)
- 1 can (14 oz) crushed tomatoes
- 1 onion, chopped
- 2 cloves garlic, minced
- ½ cup olive oil
- 1 tsp oregano
- Salt and pepper

Instructions:

1. Boil beans until tender, drain.
2. Sauté onion and garlic, add tomatoes, oil, oregano, salt, and pepper.
3. Combine beans and sauce in a baking dish, bake at 375°F (190°C) for 40 minutes.

Fasolada (Greek White Bean Soup)

Traditional Greek bean soup, simple yet hearty.

Ingredients:

- 2 cups white beans, soaked overnight
- 1 onion, chopped
- 2 carrots, sliced
- 2 celery stalks, chopped
- 1 can (14 oz) crushed tomatoes
- ¼ cup olive oil
- 1 tsp oregano
- Salt and pepper

Instructions:

1. Boil beans until tender, drain.
2. Sauté onion, carrots, and celery in olive oil.
3. Add beans, tomatoes, oregano, salt, and pepper. Simmer for 30 minutes.

Avgolemono Soup (Lemon and Egg Chicken Soup)

A creamy chicken soup thickened with eggs and flavored with lemon.

Ingredients:

- 4 cups chicken broth
- 1 cup cooked rice
- 2 eggs
- 1 lemon, juiced
- 1 cup shredded chicken
- Salt and pepper

Instructions:

1. Heat broth and add rice and chicken.
2. In a bowl, whisk eggs and lemon juice. Slowly add hot broth while whisking.
3. Pour egg mixture back into soup, stirring continuously.

Psarosoupa (Greek Fish Soup)

A light yet flavorful fish soup with vegetables.

Ingredients:

- 1 lb white fish fillets
- 4 cups fish stock or water
- 2 carrots, sliced
- 2 potatoes, cubed
- 1 onion, chopped
- 2 tbsp olive oil
- 1 lemon, juiced
- Salt and pepper

Instructions:

1. Sauté onion in olive oil. Add stock, carrots, and potatoes, simmer until tender.
2. Add fish fillets, cook for 10 minutes.
3. Stir in lemon juice, salt, and pepper.

Youvetsi (Beef or Lamb with Orzo)

A rich, slow-cooked dish with tender meat and orzo pasta.

Ingredients:

- 1 lb beef or lamb, cubed
- 1 onion, chopped
- 2 cloves garlic, minced
- 1 can (14 oz) crushed tomatoes
- ½ cup red wine
- 1 tsp cinnamon
- 1 cup orzo
- ¼ cup grated cheese (Kefalotyri or Parmesan)

Instructions:

1. Brown meat in olive oil, then sauté onion and garlic.
2. Add tomatoes, wine, cinnamon, salt, and pepper. Simmer for 1 hour.
3. Stir in orzo, cook for 10 minutes, then sprinkle with cheese.

Stifado (Greek Beef Stew with Onions)

A slow-cooked beef stew with onions and warm spices.

Ingredients:

- 1 lb beef, cubed
- 1 lb pearl onions, peeled
- 2 cloves garlic, minced
- ½ cup red wine
- 1 can (14 oz) crushed tomatoes
- 1 tbsp red wine vinegar
- 1 cinnamon stick
- 2 bay leaves

Instructions:

1. Brown beef, then sauté onions and garlic.
2. Add tomatoes, wine, vinegar, cinnamon, and bay leaves.
3. Simmer for 1.5–2 hours until tender.

Soutzoukakia (Greek Meatballs in Tomato Sauce)

Soft, spiced meatballs in a rich tomato sauce.

Ingredients:

- 1 lb ground beef
- 1 egg
- ½ cup breadcrumbs
- 2 cloves garlic, minced
- 1 tsp cumin
- 1 tsp oregano
- 1 can (14 oz) crushed tomatoes
- ½ cup red wine

Instructions:

1. Mix meat, egg, breadcrumbs, garlic, cumin, salt, and pepper. Form into meatballs.
2. Brown in olive oil, then simmer in tomatoes and wine for 30 minutes.

\

Keftedes (Greek Meatballs)

Crispy fried Greek meatballs with herbs and spices.

Ingredients:

- 1 lb ground beef or lamb
- 1 egg
- ½ cup breadcrumbs
- ½ onion, grated
- 2 tbsp chopped mint
- 1 tsp oregano
- Salt and pepper
- Olive oil for frying

Instructions:

1. Mix all ingredients and form into meatballs.
2. Fry in olive oil until golden brown.

Souvlaki (Grilled Meat Skewers)

Marinated meat skewers grilled to perfection.

Ingredients:

- 1 lb pork, chicken, or lamb, cubed
- 2 tbsp olive oil
- 1 tbsp lemon juice
- 2 cloves garlic, minced
- 1 tsp oregano
- Salt and pepper

Instructions:

1. Marinate meat in olive oil, lemon juice, garlic, oregano, salt, and pepper for 2 hours.
2. Skewer meat and grill until cooked through.

Gyros (Pita-Wrapped Meat with Tzatziki)

A Greek street food classic with spiced meat, pita, and tzatziki.

Ingredients:

- 1 lb ground lamb or beef
- 2 cloves garlic, minced
- 1 tsp oregano
- 1 tsp cumin
- Salt and pepper
- 4 pita breads
- 1 cup tzatziki sauce
- Sliced onions, tomatoes, and lettuce

Instructions:

1. Mix meat, garlic, oregano, cumin, salt, and pepper. Form into a log shape.
2. Bake at 375°F (190°C) for 40 minutes, then slice thinly.
3. Serve in pita with tzatziki, onions, tomatoes, and lettuce.

Kokkinisto (Greek Braised Meat in Tomato Sauce)

A slow-cooked meat dish with a rich, spiced tomato sauce.

Ingredients:

- 1.5 lbs beef or lamb, cubed
- 1 onion, chopped
- 2 cloves garlic, minced
- 1 can (14 oz) crushed tomatoes
- ½ cup red wine
- 1 tbsp tomato paste
- 1 tsp cinnamon
- 1 bay leaf
- Salt and pepper

Instructions:

1. Brown meat in olive oil, then sauté onion and garlic.
2. Add tomatoes, wine, tomato paste, cinnamon, bay leaf, salt, and pepper.
3. Simmer for 1.5–2 hours until tender.

Kleftiko (Slow-Cooked Lamb)

A traditional slow-roasted lamb dish with herbs and vegetables.

Ingredients:

- 2 lbs lamb shoulder
- 4 garlic cloves, minced
- 2 tbsp olive oil
- 1 lemon, juiced
- 1 tbsp oregano
- 1 tsp rosemary
- 2 potatoes, quartered
- 1 red bell pepper, sliced

Instructions:

1. Rub lamb with garlic, olive oil, lemon juice, oregano, rosemary, salt, and pepper.
2. Wrap in parchment paper with potatoes and peppers.
3. Bake at 325°F (160°C) for 3–4 hours.

Arni me Patates (Roast Lamb with Potatoes)

A simple yet flavorful Greek roast lamb dish.

Ingredients:

- 2 lbs lamb leg or shoulder
- 4 potatoes, cubed
- 4 cloves garlic, minced
- ¼ cup olive oil
- 1 tbsp oregano
- 1 lemon, juiced
- Salt and pepper

Instructions:

1. Marinate lamb and potatoes with garlic, olive oil, oregano, lemon juice, salt, and pepper.
2. Roast at 375°F (190°C) for 1.5–2 hours.

Psito Kotopoulo (Greek Roast Chicken)

A juicy, herb-marinated roasted chicken.

Ingredients:

- 1 whole chicken
- 4 cloves garlic, minced
- ¼ cup olive oil
- 2 tbsp lemon juice
- 1 tbsp oregano
- 1 tsp paprika
- Salt and pepper

Instructions:

1. Rub chicken with garlic, olive oil, lemon juice, oregano, paprika, salt, and pepper.
2. Roast at 375°F (190°C) for 1.5 hours.

Bakaliaros Skordalia (Fried Cod with Garlic Sauce)

A crispy fried cod dish with a creamy garlic potato sauce.

Ingredients:

- 1 lb cod fillets
- ½ cup flour
- ½ cup sparkling water
- Salt and pepper
- Olive oil for frying

For Skordalia:

- 2 boiled potatoes
- 4 garlic cloves
- ¼ cup olive oil
- 2 tbsp vinegar
- Salt

Instructions:

1. Mix flour, water, salt, and pepper. Dip cod and fry until golden.
2. Mash potatoes with garlic, olive oil, vinegar, and salt for Skordalia sauce.

Xtapodi Stifado (Octopus Stew)

A tender octopus stew with a rich tomato sauce.

Ingredients:

- 1 lb octopus, cleaned and cut into pieces
- 1 onion, chopped
- 2 cloves garlic, minced
- 1 can (14 oz) crushed tomatoes
- ½ cup red wine
- 1 bay leaf
- 1 tsp cinnamon
- Salt and pepper

Instructions:

1. Sauté octopus until it releases liquid.
2. Add onions, garlic, tomatoes, wine, bay leaf, cinnamon, salt, and pepper.
3. Simmer for 1.5 hours.

Garides Saganaki (Shrimp in Tomato and Feta Sauce)

A flavorful shrimp dish with tomatoes and feta cheese.

Ingredients:

- 1 lb shrimp, peeled
- 1 can (14 oz) crushed tomatoes
- 2 cloves garlic, minced
- ½ cup white wine
- ¼ tsp red pepper flakes
- ½ cup feta cheese, crumbled
- 2 tbsp olive oil

Instructions:

1. Sauté garlic in olive oil, add tomatoes, wine, and pepper flakes. Simmer.
2. Add shrimp, cook for 5 minutes, then top with feta.

Midia Saganaki (Mussels in Tomato and Feta Sauce)

A rich and spicy mussel dish with feta cheese.

Ingredients:

- 1 lb mussels, cleaned
- 1 can (14 oz) crushed tomatoes
- 2 cloves garlic, minced
- ½ cup white wine
- ½ cup feta cheese, crumbled
- 2 tbsp olive oil

Instructions:

1. Sauté garlic in olive oil, add tomatoes and wine. Simmer.
2. Add mussels, cover, and cook until they open.
3. Top with feta.

Briam (Greek Ratatouille)

A baked vegetable dish full of Mediterranean flavors.

Ingredients:

- 1 eggplant, sliced
- 2 zucchini, sliced
- 2 potatoes, sliced
- 1 onion, sliced
- 1 can (14 oz) crushed tomatoes
- ¼ cup olive oil
- 1 tsp oregano

Instructions:

1. Layer vegetables in a baking dish.
2. Pour over tomatoes, olive oil, and oregano.
3. Bake at 375°F (190°C) for 45 minutes.

Imam Bayildi (Stuffed Eggplant)

A rich, slow-cooked eggplant stuffed with onions and tomatoes.

Ingredients:

- 2 eggplants, halved
- 1 onion, sliced
- 2 cloves garlic, minced
- 1 can (14 oz) crushed tomatoes
- ¼ cup olive oil
- 1 tsp cinnamon

Instructions:

1. Sauté onions and garlic, mix with tomatoes and cinnamon.
2. Stuff eggplants with mixture and bake at 375°F (190°C) for 45 minutes.

Gemista (Stuffed Tomatoes and Peppers)

A classic dish of tomatoes and peppers filled with rice and herbs.

Ingredients:

- 4 tomatoes
- 4 bell peppers
- 1 cup rice
- 1 onion, chopped
- 2 tbsp olive oil
- ½ cup fresh herbs (dill, mint, parsley)

Instructions:

1. Hollow out tomatoes and peppers, save pulp.
2. Mix rice, onion, herbs, olive oil, and pulp. Stuff vegetables.
3. Bake at 375°F (190°C) for 1 hour.

Fasolia Yiahni (Braised Green Beans in Tomato Sauce)

A comforting dish of green beans slow-cooked in tomato sauce.

Ingredients:

- 1 lb green beans
- 1 onion, chopped
- 2 cloves garlic, minced
- 1 can (14 oz) crushed tomatoes
- ¼ cup olive oil
- 1 tsp oregano

Instructions:

1. Sauté onion and garlic in olive oil.
2. Add tomatoes, green beans, oregano, salt, and pepper.
3. Simmer for 30–40 minutes.

Horta Vrasta (Boiled Wild Greens with Olive Oil and Lemon)

A simple, nutritious dish featuring boiled greens with olive oil and lemon.

Ingredients:

- 1 lb wild greens (dandelion, chicory, or spinach)
- 1 lemon, juiced
- 3 tbsp olive oil
- Salt

Instructions:

1. Wash greens thoroughly.
2. Boil in salted water for 10 minutes until tender.
3. Drain and drizzle with olive oil and lemon juice before serving.

Revithia Sto Fourno (Baked Chickpeas)

A comforting, slow-baked chickpea dish with olive oil and herbs.

Ingredients:

- 2 cups dried chickpeas, soaked overnight
- 1 onion, chopped
- 2 cloves garlic, minced
- 1/4 cup olive oil
- 1 tsp oregano
- 1 lemon, juiced
- Salt and pepper

Instructions:

1. Drain chickpeas and place in a baking dish.
2. Add onion, garlic, olive oil, oregano, lemon juice, salt, and pepper.
3. Add enough water to cover and bake at 350°F (175°C) for 2–3 hours until tender.

Melomakarona (Honey-Dipped Spiced Cookies)

Soft, spiced cookies soaked in honey syrup and topped with walnuts.

Ingredients:

- 3 ½ cups flour
- 1 cup olive oil
- ½ cup orange juice
- ½ cup sugar
- 1 tsp cinnamon
- ½ tsp baking soda

For syrup:

- 1 cup honey
- ½ cup water
- ½ cup sugar

Instructions:

1. Mix flour, olive oil, orange juice, sugar, cinnamon, and baking soda.
2. Shape into small ovals and bake at 350°F (175°C) for 20 minutes.
3. Boil honey, water, and sugar for syrup. Dip warm cookies in syrup and top with chopped walnuts.

Kourabiedes (Greek Butter Cookies with Powdered Sugar)

Rich, buttery cookies covered in powdered sugar.

Ingredients:

- 1 cup butter, softened
- ½ cup powdered sugar
- 2 cups flour
- ½ cup almonds, chopped
- 1 tsp vanilla extract
- Extra powdered sugar for coating

Instructions:

1. Cream butter and sugar, then add flour, almonds, and vanilla.
2. Shape into small rounds and bake at 350°F (175°C) for 20 minutes.
3. Cool and roll in powdered sugar.

Loukoumades (Greek Honey Puffs)

Crispy, fried dough balls drizzled with honey and cinnamon.

Ingredients:

- 2 cups flour
- 1 packet yeast
- 1 cup warm water
- ½ tsp salt
- Oil for frying

For topping:

- ½ cup honey
- 1 tsp cinnamon

Instructions:

1. Mix flour, yeast, water, and salt to form a batter. Let rise for 1 hour.
2. Fry spoonfuls in hot oil until golden.
3. Drizzle with honey and sprinkle with cinnamon.

Baklava (Layered Phyllo Pastry with Nuts and Honey)

A classic Greek dessert with flaky phyllo, spiced nuts, and sweet syrup.

Ingredients:

- 1 pack phyllo dough
- 2 cups walnuts, chopped
- 1 cup butter, melted
- 1 tsp cinnamon

For syrup:

- 1 cup honey
- ½ cup sugar
- ½ cup water

Instructions:

1. Layer phyllo sheets in a baking dish, brushing each with butter.
2. Sprinkle chopped walnuts and cinnamon every few layers.
3. Bake at 350°F (175°C) for 45 minutes.
4. Boil honey, sugar, and water for syrup. Pour over baklava while hot.

Galaktoboureko (Custard Phyllo Pie)

A creamy semolina custard baked in crispy phyllo and soaked in syrup.

Ingredients:

- 1 pack phyllo dough
- 1 cup butter, melted
- 4 cups milk
- ½ cup semolina
- ½ cup sugar
- 3 eggs
- 1 tsp vanilla

For syrup:

- 1 cup sugar
- ½ cup water
- ½ cup honey

Instructions:

1. Heat milk and add semolina, sugar, and vanilla. Let cool slightly.
2. Stir in beaten eggs and mix well.
3. Layer phyllo sheets in a baking dish, brushing each with butter. Pour in custard and top with more phyllo.
4. Bake at 350°F (175°C) for 45 minutes.
5. Boil sugar, water, and honey for syrup. Pour over baked pie.

Bougatsa (Greek Custard or Cheese Pastry)

A phyllo pastry filled with custard or cheese, dusted with sugar and cinnamon.

Ingredients:

- 1 pack phyllo dough
- 1 cup butter, melted
- 4 cups milk
- ½ cup semolina
- ½ cup sugar
- 2 eggs
- 1 tsp vanilla

Instructions:

1. Heat milk and add semolina, sugar, and vanilla. Stir until thick.
2. Stir in beaten eggs and let cool.
3. Layer phyllo in a baking dish, adding butter between layers. Pour in filling and top with more phyllo.
4. Bake at 350°F (175°C) for 40 minutes.
5. Dust with powdered sugar and cinnamon before serving.

Kataifi (Shredded Phyllo Dessert with Nuts and Syrup)

A crispy, syrup-soaked dessert made with shredded phyllo dough and spiced nuts.

Ingredients:

- 1 pack kataifi dough (shredded phyllo)
- 2 cups walnuts, chopped
- 1 cup butter, melted
- 1 tsp cinnamon

For syrup:

- 1 cup honey
- ½ cup sugar
- ½ cup water

Instructions:

1. Spread kataifi dough on a baking dish. Mix nuts and cinnamon and sprinkle over.
2. Roll or fold dough over filling, then brush with butter.
3. Bake at 350°F (175°C) for 40 minutes.
4. Boil honey, sugar, and water for syrup. Pour over kataifi while hot.

Rizogalo (Greek Rice Pudding)

A creamy, comforting dessert with cinnamon and vanilla.

Ingredients:

- ½ cup short-grain rice
- 2 cups water
- 4 cups milk
- ½ cup sugar
- 1 tsp vanilla extract
- 1 tbsp cornstarch (optional, for thickness)
- Cinnamon for garnish

Instructions:

1. Rinse rice and boil in water until soft.
2. Add milk and sugar, stirring frequently. Simmer for 15 minutes.
3. If needed, dissolve cornstarch in 2 tbsp cold milk and stir into the pudding.
4. Remove from heat, add vanilla, and mix well.
5. Serve warm or chilled, topped with cinnamon.

Halva (Semolina or Tahini-Based Dessert)

A simple, sweet dessert often flavored with nuts and spices.

Ingredients:

- 1 cup semolina
- ½ cup olive oil or butter
- 1 cup sugar
- 2 cups water
- 1 tsp cinnamon
- ½ cup chopped walnuts or almonds

Instructions:

1. In a pot, heat olive oil and toast semolina until golden brown.
2. In another pot, boil water and sugar until syrupy.
3. Slowly pour syrup into semolina while stirring.
4. Add cinnamon and nuts, mix, and let cool before serving.

Portokalopita (Orange Phyllo Cake)

A moist, fragrant orange cake made with crumbled phyllo dough.

Ingredients:

- 1 pack phyllo dough, shredded
- 4 eggs
- 1 cup sugar
- 1 cup Greek yogurt
- 1 cup vegetable oil
- 1 tbsp baking powder
- Zest of 2 oranges

For syrup:

- 1 cup sugar
- 1 cup orange juice
- ½ cup water

Instructions:

1. Preheat oven to 350°F (175°C).
2. Whisk eggs, sugar, yogurt, oil, baking powder, and orange zest.
3. Add shredded phyllo and mix well.
4. Pour into a greased pan and bake for 40 minutes.
5. Boil syrup ingredients and pour over cake while hot.

Tsoureki (Greek Sweet Bread)

A soft, aromatic Easter bread with mahleb and mastiha spices.

Ingredients:

- 4 cups flour
- 1 cup warm milk
- ½ cup sugar
- 2 eggs
- 1 tbsp yeast
- 1 tsp mahleb (optional)
- ½ tsp mastiha (optional)
- ½ cup butter, melted

Instructions:

1. Mix yeast with warm milk and a bit of sugar. Let sit for 10 minutes.
2. Add eggs, sugar, mahleb, and mastiha. Mix in flour and knead for 10 minutes.
3. Let dough rise for 2 hours. Shape into braids and let rise again.
4. Brush with egg wash and bake at 350°F (175°C) for 30 minutes.

Diples (Fried Pastry with Honey and Nuts)

A crispy, honey-drizzled dessert often made for celebrations.

Ingredients:

- 2 cups flour
- 2 eggs
- 1 tbsp sugar
- 1 tbsp brandy
- Oil for frying

For topping:

- ½ cup honey
- ½ cup chopped walnuts
- 1 tsp cinnamon

Instructions:

1. Mix flour, eggs, sugar, and brandy into a dough. Let rest for 30 minutes.
2. Roll dough thin, cut into strips, and fry until golden.
3. Drizzle with warm honey and sprinkle with walnuts and cinnamon.

Karydopita (Greek Walnut Cake with Syrup)

A rich, spiced walnut cake soaked in syrup.

Ingredients:

- 2 cups walnuts, chopped
- 1 cup flour
- 1 cup sugar
- 1 tsp baking powder
- 1 tsp cinnamon
- 4 eggs
- ½ cup butter, melted

For syrup:

- 1 cup sugar
- 1 cup water
- ½ cup honey

Instructions:

1. Mix flour, walnuts, sugar, baking powder, and cinnamon.
2. Beat eggs and add to dry ingredients. Mix in butter.
3. Bake at 350°F (175°C) for 30 minutes.
4. Boil syrup ingredients and pour over hot cake.

Avgofetes (Greek-Style French Toast)

A crispy, sweet French toast variation with honey and cinnamon.

Ingredients:

- 4 slices of bread
- 2 eggs
- ½ cup milk
- ½ tsp cinnamon
- ½ tsp vanilla
- Butter for frying

For topping:

- ¼ cup honey
- ½ tsp cinnamon

Instructions:

1. Whisk eggs, milk, cinnamon, and vanilla.
2. Dip bread slices and fry in butter until golden.
3. Drizzle with honey and sprinkle with cinnamon.

Ouzo Spritz (Greek Aperitif Cocktail)

A refreshing, bubbly ouzo-based cocktail.

Ingredients:

- 2 oz ouzo
- 3 oz soda water
- 1 oz fresh lemon juice
- Ice cubes
- Lemon slices for garnish

Instructions:

1. Fill a glass with ice.
2. Pour ouzo, lemon juice, and soda water.
3. Stir gently and garnish with lemon slices.

Ellinikos Kafes (Traditional Greek Coffee)

A strong, unfiltered coffee served with foam on top.

Ingredients:

- 1 cup cold water
- 1 heaping tsp Greek coffee
- 1 tsp sugar (optional)

Instructions:

1. Add water, coffee, and sugar (if using) to a briki (Greek coffee pot).
2. Heat slowly without stirring until foam rises.
3. Pour into a cup and let grounds settle before drinking.

www.ingramcontent.com/pod-product-compliance
Lightning Source LLC
LaVergne TN
LVHW081338060526
838201LV00055B/2721